Organizing the Diaspora

Aframericanism, Volume 1

Piankh Piankh

Published by Piankh, 2024.

ORGANIZING THE DIASPORA

First edition. January 1, 2024.

ISBN: 978-1637951064

Written by Piankh Piankh.

Also by Piankh Piankh

Aframericanism
Organizing the Diaspora

Standalone
A Short Treatise on the Space-Time Continuum
Reconstruction: African American

Preface

The black populations of the Americas are lamenting the social and economic conditions of their communities while nearly all of them plot an escape route to a better sphere of existence; away from themselves. It is everyone for himself and herself. Community is disparaged in all but name.

The purpose of this essay is to lay out some essential points as a foundation for a viable Black survival in the Americas. This is the second decade of the twenty first century. In our age all problems are attended to scientifically, if they are worthy of serious attention.

Black people must become scientific about their social issues and stay away from sentimentality. The whole body of science is a set of continuous debates: collecting of data; comparison of data; formulation of theory; testing and implementation. Because we are dealing with people and contrary people, we will need to not only be clever but devious in approaching solutions to our problems. This is the ultimate work, the work of survival, what is it we will not do?

In our age all legitimate political change is democratic. Black people will have to develop democratic processes to implement social changes among themselves. This will be a question of intellect and opportunity.

This is my seminal work. It took a whole lifetime to reach the conclusions that I have written here. Between the ages of sixteen and twenty-one I served a five-year engineering apprenticeship and later graduate from university with honors degree in Physics. In youth my main past time was reading ancient history; there is a lot of sociology in ancient history and religion. It is like five thousand years of experimentation.

Consider a man whose home was destroyed by a hurricane. Everyone would think him a fool, if he sits on a stump among the rubble and say he is waiting for the hurricane to rebuild it. The process of history has destroyed the social bearings of Africans in the Americas. We must rebuild. The development cannot be revolutionary, it must be democratic and because of universal education this may be the first time in history when it is possible for the general people to reform themselves by their own intellect. I am putting forward here, the farthest outline of the debate. The debate must be conducted in the public by the people, among themselves and their conclusions recorded and codified as "their" formal rules of conduct.

I have contended with many from the man in the street and found that when his prejudices are put aside, common sense is good enough to lead him to the answer. My indebtedness to those interactions and those people, too many to name, is considerable. I thank them for enduring my invasive queries. One gentleman stands out in my mind, named Herschel and I still get a chuckle on remembering his comments. Unable to see the possibilities I kept repeating, he dubbed me, 'the man from La Mancha'.

The essential points of the article are found in the principles of social action. Who so ever that have a program, a project or a philosophy they say will lead to Aframerican communal advancement let them declare where they stand on these five principles: then we will know where they are really going.

Preamble.

Overview: organizing the diaspora

Those who engage in debate or put forth reasoned arguments of necessity take some things for granted. They assume an unspoken agreement on the very rudimentary elements of their concerns; often this is not the case, especially in social issues. This very great debate on Aframerican salvation is been waged in countless venues from the halls academia to street corners and halls where Captain Morgan is arbiter. The debates are numerous and the under pinnings of these debates are equally numerous, depending on religious conviction, local history, political conviction, family disposition, education and all kinds of whims according to individual sentiments. Consequently, the debate is not advancing. There needs to be known threads of the debate anchored by known beliefs or facts. That way anyone who is interested can pick up the thread and follow it in either direction.

The principles of social action annunciated here are founded on some salient points of human reality. That reality is easily perceived differently so it is important to say what they are. The position taken on these issues can be considered as just beliefs, although some effort is made to justify them. They are presented from the position of an observer striving diligently to be neutral, detached, and scientific in all respects except a desire for development of a system of Aframerican salvation.

Some Aspects of Society

Humanity, as we know it, is fractured into thousands of pieces, each harboring antagonisms, some of which go back several millennia. The ill will is always there and can produce violence on a scale ranging from injury to a single individual to global warfare resulting in the deaths of tens of millions. This generation of humanity inherited these divisions and is not able to do much about the situation. The trouble that would result from trying to reorder the world would be horrific. For the foreseeable future humanity will exist in competing parts often trying to eliminate each other.

Human societies are not benign aggregates of people doing their own thing, they are competitive devices designed to counteract other humans; as such, they constitute massive conspiracies . The individuals inside a community are only individuals to a limited degree. They are born as human animals then they put forth their best (may be greatest effort) to fit themselves into a system, and by the time they become aware; they are agents of the system.

Any community that allows its new recruits to be inducted into another system would promptly cease to exist. For going against social norms individuals are ostracized, excommunicated, or executed. Besides been aware of these possibilities, the average individual will not have any desire to go against the norm because he/she is an adjunct of the system-the norm.

Societies do not all originate at the same time, they do not evolve at the same rate, have not had the same experiences; consequently, some are quite sophisticated-advanced, while others are quite simple-primitive. Aframerican societies are primitive. They simply have not had time to develop the proper responses to normal challenges that communities face. Unfortunately, they are in the thick of the fray struggling against the best.

The social methods (techniques, technologies) by which societies implement their agenda can be transferred from one to the other. Hence, societies can learn without having to go through the same learning process. This apparently is quite difficult because not many societies do it without great trauma.

Aframerican Social Condition and Identity

Aframerican contemporary social conditions and methods are the results of practices and conditions forcibly maintained among them when they were in bondage. These conditions were kept up long enough that they became the internal norms of their communities. Because of this history, Aframericans have been completely defined by their chief competition in the Americas. Irrespective of the nature of the contest, this is a losing position to be in.

Since the 1960's, social analyst had concluded that Aframericans were dehumanized while in bondage and this had become the fashionable notion for explaining their condition. The popular response to this idea is that the people who dehumanized them should create a permanent leeway for them. This approach, whatever merits and attraction it may have, left the ultimate responsibility for Aframerican survival in the hands of their chief competitor. No individual or community in their right mind would do this.

Every Aframerican community is a degenerate version of a corresponding European community. Besides been culturally divided into desperate fragments that mirror the cultural diversity of Western Europe; Aframericans also bear a genetic heritage reflecting the people diversity of Western Europe. There is within this admixture an underlying African strain but in a high percent of cases this is quite marginal. There is, therefore, within the concept of an Aframerican people, many legitimate but conflicting loyalties and aspirations.

The normal tribal community, from which all present communities came, (except Aframerican) has built into its apparatus responses which are equivalent to the foreign policy of the territorial state. The people within these states are the same and their attitudes to outsiders are the same as when they lived by themselves as a tribe. Aframerican response to outside influences developed under the auspices of outsiders who had a negative interest in Aframerican progress. Consequently, the latter has remained susceptible to exploitation by outsiders and opposed to any form of internal synchronism.

A people's identity is more often than not inextricably tied up with their modus operandi. They see themselves as the people who do this, that or the other, whatever is their particular set of practices. In most instances of tribal divisions around the world the people can only be distinguished by their practices any way. People are inclined to feel, therefore, that changing their social practices will threaten their social existence. Numerous instances of such changes since the industrial revolution are proof that their sentiments are unfounded. Here are two instances: although both Japan and South Korea have adapted the sociology and technology of industrialism, mostly developed in Great Britain, no one visiting these countries would mistake them for England, human physiology aside. Identity will become a core issue around which all other aspects of Aframerican salvation are likely to revolve. If this does not occur, then we will have a set of people attempting to organize "something," but not knowing what it is.

There has been no successful reform in any Aframerican community. The management of the territorial state concentrates its efforts on macroeconomics and law and order, clearly indispensable elements of society, but there is something else going on that is impervious to their best efforts.

The constitutions that define the territorial state and order its management do not say anything about the underlying society; it is taken for granted that a viable, functioning society exists. If, as in Aframerican communities, the underlying society tends to self-destruct (a countervailing culture) or to append itself as a marginal subgroup to another community, then all the best effort of the best economic specialist will come to naught.

Aframericans are essentially various groups of outcast people who have been lumped together by historical processes beyond their control and appear to have formed communities. They cannot, individually or in groups, join other communities; otherwise the whole Aframerican phenomena would vanish. This makes them a permanent grouping. Aframericans are a people in formation and their affairs could be resolved in thousands of different ways depending on their wisdom and the environment. Their communities will be subject to competitive forces of all the world's people vying among themselves to make a living in the Americas, and they will be pulverized and mesmerized unless they develop (acquire) systems of actions and responses equivalent to the competition.

Extent of Competition

Competition among people is all pervasive and at all levels. All human beings live in communities and they compete most intensely at that level. This is evidenced by the fact that most homicides are a result of war, not individual violence. In general, people are not portable between communities; if they were, many communities would vanish. Individuals cannot walk out of one community and join another as they see fit. Call this phenomenon whatever you like, there are not many places in the world where it is a common thing. It does not matter the arena; whether it is in exam scores, in finding oil deposits, fishing grounds, mathematical theories or the analysis of DNA structures, communities that fail to keep up are going to be marginalized and certain consequences follow. The effects may take generations or even centuries to become evident. It must be borne in mind that we are dealing with entities that endure for thousands of years and the considerations need to have that kind of scope, or at least needs to reach for it. Aframericans are in a struggle for survival; not for a piece of cake, not just for better jobs, or better housing, etc., but for life itself. These are not activities that people choose to be in; they are consequences of being alive.

Systems of Competition

The competition faced by Aframericans is similar to that faced by many groups around the world; the main difference is likely to be the severity of Aframerican social deficiency because they are a brand new people created by the processes of the industrial revolution. On the other hand, the opposition consists of various groups organized to compete as exclusive communities and to preserve their identity at all cost. This, they have been doing in some instances, for well over 4,000 years. Note that with the loss of identity, the game is over.

Around the world there are numerous groups (communities) that are minorities, but were once the major people in their region, even in the world, leaders in art and science. Since ancient times there is some process going on in their society that causes them to be losing ground to the competition. In some cases, the competition has adopted their social methods (technologies) and modified them. Sometimes they may have been losing ground at an equivalent rate of a few percent per century, but over a thousand years this becomes a disaster. On the other hand, there are other groups of people who quite happily move around the world seeking opportunities and easily take over host communities where the locals do make laws against it. There are so many examples, globally, where the same groups of people turn up in the same strata of a host community, the phenomenon has got to be a function of their own internal mechanisms.

To the degree that Aframericans are immersed in the regiments of their culture and cannot escape without great trauma, so are their competitors. The processes by which they overwhelm other communities and marginalize them did not originate with the present generation. The present generation is likely to think they are the guardians of a great success formula and has no incentive to change it. The onus is on the losing side to adapt to suit the demands of life and to survive.

Faced with such an array of illustrious combatants, Aframericans may feel daunted but it must be borne in mind that it is always a contest of system versus system, and although individuals are the ultimate actors, they are pouring into and out of these systems in streams of endless millions; the systems endure and continue their functions regardless. Most importantly, systems can be devised, copied, adopted, and adapted.

Image and Contest

Among human beings, self-image and the concept of image in general is of great and growing significance. The way individuals, groups, communities and nations perceive themselves and are perceived by others is a phenomenon that is actively attended to by all people who understand this aspect of humanity. Nations go to war and lose thousands of lives just to make sure they are not perceived wrongly. Individuals at their level behave in a similar manner. The image of corporeal humanity, although it is quite ethereal and untouchable, seems to suffer from all the shortcomings of its origin; it can be attacked and destroyed. Therefore, it needs to be protected and promoted. Promoting an image is like feeding an animal. If a people do not promote their image, it will wither and die, and they will follow after it. It is to be noted that "a people" is quite an ethereal entity too.

The struggle is taking place on all levels of human existence including such ethereal domains as spirituality. There is an intense and increasingly subtle contest been waged in those fields. These are areas where primitive peoples seem to lose before they begin. They behave as if it is all passing over their heads. In the struggle for survival there are no holds barred; people can borrow methods and means, even the competitor's identity may be borrowed, but a people who losses their own identity in the process have lost.

The Future

Competition is not about to go way, but instead will intensify as we go forward with more internationalization and globalization. We will expect fewer major wars in the future, but the effects of the lower-level competition will be the same; some people are going to lose their homelands, and some will cease to exist altogether. This is not new but some of the procedures are different. Individuals who hate war and violence will fail to see the same consequences resulting from the normal commercial relationships that we live with. The case is arguable, but the latter situation may give the losing sides a better chance to adjust. The free enterprise system has made the competition global. In many parts of the world people often fail to see the big picture and identify only their local competitors. A cane cutter in Jamaica, West Indies, who may be illiterate, finds himself competing against cane cutters in Borneo or Bangladesh or Botswana, who also may be illiterate.

There is competition among human beings at all levels at which they operate, and they are not required to interact directly in any of the fields in which the performance is relevant. As countries compete against each other, sometimes the upper hand is gained by the country with the more effective education system; sometimes by the country with more productive workers; sometimes by the country with the more healthy workers; or sometimes with happier workers and so on. The fields of intense activity are likely to move around arbitrarily just as above. This same scenario applies to all the countries that the United States or Japan compete with. Everybody is involved. Even the people who are living in their forests, blissfully unaware of a teeming globe of anxious humanity, daily making wrenching decisions on their future, are having their air polluted and depleted, their water poison and sky obscured.

Everything that comes into the purview of man is sooner or later pressed into service in aid of survival. Consider the religions based on various concept of god. From the most ancient times of recorded history people have deployed their religious practices with an aim to gain advantage in commerce, in war or in love. The religions generally do not object; on the contrary some of them are virtually based on the idea of gaining an upper hand through religious devotion.

The struggle for life on earth is likely to become increasingly subtle as more of life's needs are produced by machines. The advanced communities will have greater production surpluses and easily able to support larger marginal populations. Humanism will also propagate globally with the spread of industrialism, thus making it emotionally acceptable for people to help others. The marginal peoples will be befuddled by this behavior; their image will suffer, they will become dispirited, and over a period of time they commit suicide. We say they die out. They are in fact rubbed out by degrees, imperceptibly, and they themselves do not know of a definite time when anything specific happened to cause their abolition. This is happening to Aframericans everywhere in the western world at the beginning of the 21st century.

Issue of Democracy

In our age no person in his or her right mind disagrees with the basic beliefs of democracy: which is that all individuals have the same sovereign powers in the management of their own affairs. As it turns out, an individual's affairs are quite extensive. They live in a city or town and share the streets, the water, the air, the birds, and many other amenities with other correspondingly powerful individuals. Strange as it may seem, the original consensual system for managing these affairs has been monarchial government.

Monarchy was the most common mode of government of humanity for over 5,000 years, and this is most likely because it was most effective. The Europeans trace their democracy to ancient Greece and oft mentioned in the process that those Greeks did not practice representative democracy as we do and actually gave up the idea in favor of monarchy. The Greeks have a king to this day. In fact, democracy may not be a system that is absolutely good for humanity, but a system for which the time has come. That time may have been determined by population, material technologies, and maybe just the weight of history.

The "avant-garde" social movement (democracy) that is sweeping the world is in fact a West European system of consensus. In general, many people had evolved various forms of consensus long before with differing level of participation. In some communities a council of elders votes for the election of the king. There was not this great emphasis on the common man, anywhere. This is not, obviously, a good thing. The common man is easily manipulated by those who know how to do it. In the Americas, democracy is truly plebeian because they historically were distant from monarchies of Europe. Somewhat like the field of popular music, ideas championed for social action varies from the lewd and crude to the sublime. In spite of this apparent banality, democracy as we know it today in the West has solid philosophical foundations and the imprint of some of the most distinguished thinkers of Western Europe over the last four centuries. Besides there has been much lost of life and anguish wrought in its defense, directly and indirectly. There is no turning back this clock; democratic processes will be the Aframerican mode of proceeding.

In a democracy all rights belong to the majority. A majority in its right mind would make laws and interpret them so as to benefit from them. The majority would find reasons (natural reasons, in its thinking) for changing the laws or the interpretation if the current goes against it. The majority, however they see themselves, do not need any malign intent in order to do this. This is comparable to any other competitive situation, like a game, any game, in the middle of play one tries the best to adapt to the wiles of the adversary. We are going to assume that the majority is always in its right mind.

Everywhere in the Americas where there are any significant economic activities, the Aframerican is a minority, sometimes a tiny minority, immersed in a population that is dynamic, aggressive, and often antagonistic, pursuing their own interest via numerous channels. (Economic, social, cultural, legal, illegal, legislative, conspiratorial, etc.) Under these conditions Aframerican interest will only advance incidentally; they will continue to be marginalized without end and consequently frustrated without end.

In order to survive and advance its interest the Aframerican needs to plot and plan, connive and contrive and conspire. All these maneuverings are the everyday fare of the many communities (peoples) who have survived for thousands of years. To them, strategizing and social maneuverings are natural reflexes, and however hard times become, they find a way through it, round it, under it and make it to the next level and it is all community work. The practitioners do not need to know explicitly what they are doing. They mostly do not and generally just place faith in what they are doing because the methods have gotten them so far. Aframericans, unfortunately, are starting this process from scratch.

This is a competitive situation; it always was, and it always will be. It follows, therefore, that no competitor who can help it would give over his fate to the control of a fellow competitor, neither benign nor malign. In order to take control of their destiny, under the current rules of play, which is popular democracy, the Aframerican must maneuver to gain numerical advantages in those places in the Americas where it is practical to do so. There are places where it would be possible to do this with little effort and others where it would take some time. Aframericans need to have an adaptive system of leadership that is in the people, and consequently emerges among them whenever a group of them is formed. The machinations of other communities are likely to bring disadvantages to Aframericans. It is a certainty they will act to promote their well-being because that is their normal mode of operation. There is a saying, "if you are not planning to succeed, then you are planning to fail." If Aframericans do not develop a system of success then they will fail consistently. Ultimately, the contest will be system versus system, and there will be high performers and low performers, but there is no law of nature that says the latter must be Aframerican.

Introduction

A Crisis

It is widely accepted that there is a crisis in the African American community. Enactment of the civil rights laws of 1964 was for the African American the dawn of a new era. In the ensuing period they lived with renewed hope and expectations. After the passage of some 30 years it has become clear to many that these expectations have not been fulfilled and are not about to become so. This occurs amidst a general movement in the majority population to undo the legal framework created then to adjust the social relationships in the country. These prescribed relationships were employed by many officials, using the apparatus of the state to keep African Americans in their place, which was similar to or even worst than when slavery was practiced.

The African Americans and many other people, individually and in their groups, resisted these institutions and prevailed, but the conditions they had caused seems at times to be set in stone, defying many creative efforts to bring some kind of parity between the African Americans and their contemporaries.

Since the civil rights era, a number of euphemisms have come into popular usage along with some behavioral changes that are clearly indicative of good intentions, but there is a major outcry for something else. Now we hardly hear of colored people, and Negroes, master race and inferior race. Instead we use ethnic minority and majority, the poor, the deprived, socially dysfunctional, etc. All this is good and in the right direction, but on the other hand the socio-economic conditions and relationships that inspired the civil rights movement have not changed in African American favor. There has been considerable improvement in various aspects of their lifestyles, but across the board the gap between them and their host community has worsened in every indicator that is of social concern. Since the early 1990's, communal leadership, both in and out of the African American population, has proclaimed a crisis in the community

This situation naturally stirs concerned people to action. As a result there has been conferences, marches, meetings, and much analyses and writings on the matter, but most of what has been done will eventually end up by-passing the problem, and this will not be known until another 30 years has passed. That there are serious problems is widely accepted, but on the nature or origins and the solutions they invoke there is no consensus. That a crisis should emerge in spite of the best efforts of some of the most well intentioned people of this era should impel this generation to leave no stone unturned in our search for an understanding of this situation; and especially in light of the fact that our labors will not bear recognizable fruit for over a generation. The solution or solutions to any problem is within the detailed delineation of the problem itself. We must develop a process to define the situation and propagate a popular, controlled debate, free from animosities and sentiments.

Extent of the Crisis

The success of the American civil rights movement has echoed throughout the western world, particularly in the more advanced countries. It is not popularly recognized in the United States that the civil rights movement was part of a global de-colonization process that ensued at the end of the Second World War. In many writings and speeches, prominent leaders of the time, referred to the Negro population as an internal colony of the United States. The problems of black America run across the board for all the African related populations in the western hemisphere. The same social ills plagued them 30 years ago and the same social deterioration runs through their communities in the 1990's, and now into the 21st century. None of these groups has emerged from colonization manifesting the spirit of the age, ready to join in the processes that characterize activities of the modern nations. Socio-economic parity is not about to emerge between the African Diaspora and any of their contemporary neighbors in the west. Therefore, when one takes a step back, it can be seen that there is an Afro-Pan-American crisis, not just a crisis of the USA Blacks.

The various groups of African derived people in the Americas have had very similar historical experience in the western world and are generally referred to collectively as the African Diaspora. This reference, the African Diaspora, invokes connotations of various peoples vaguely related by an African connection and beyond that nothing. In the introduction to his book, Sex and Race, J. A. Rogers described the people whom he is writing about and called them Aframerican (Afra-merican).

Aframerican implies a people, a nation, or a nationalist movement. If we are to impact history (the future), then we must begin at some point to pull our desperate ends together. This name begins the process by recognizing that these people, who were Africans, but are now quite disconnected from that continent, form an integral, discernible part of historical movements in the Americas.

J.A. Rogers was a tireless worker in the Aframerican cause, his literary works were a masterful initiation of Aframerican history, and we follow his lead. He was a contemporary of Marcus Garvey. The latter believed Aframerican problems were solvable and set about to implement his ideas. History has recorded the results. Since his time, we have had over 100 years of accumulated experience, tremendous scholarship, transformed and improved socio-economic technologies, but a worsened situation to deal with. Marcus Garvey tackled the African problems on a global scale with little or non-existent means; in addition, he had major opposition. His most significant impact was psychological. A foreigner in the United States of America, he toiled on behalf of all Aframericans without regard for national origin or religion. Naturally, Marcus Garvey is the foremost Aframerican.

At the end of the Second World War, large numbers of people thought they had learned something about how all human beings should live. Great things had been achieved and much of the world imagined we could do better in the future. From this point we embarked on the most exciting period in human history to date, pursuing the most thrilling adventures. Intellectually, this has being a most fulfilling and rewarding time for mankind. Unfortunately, it has also been just about the most frustrating era in the history of African communities everywhere, but especially in Africa.

Since the 1960's, the situation in Africa went from jubilant hope to dissolution and desperation in the 1990's. Therefore, what we have is a global crisis of people related to Africa. The Aframerican is not organized to operate on a global scale, not even in local affairs are there any Aframerican capabilities to be deployed regionally. In this search for African survival, Aframericans can best help by first righting themselves; put their priority efforts into Aframerican rehabilitation and create a movement to enact it. Marcus Garvey's grand vision for the African people was completely thwarted, and we are left still at the beginning, dreaming of independent, viable Aframerican nations with all the trappings of modern states. Toward that end we need a system of Aframerican survival, able to cope with contemporary competitive systems and any others that may arise in the future. This would only come about as the result of a process. This then is the clearest responsibility for this generation: create and initiate a reiterative process leading to Aframerican salvation.

The Variables

Contemporary Aframerican reform efforts are aimed at improved standard of living, reduction of crime, and better inter-communal relations. These are noble quests that most people desire; the problem arises in deciding how to go about creating the reality. The variables effecting Aframerican life may be divided into two sets, internal and external. They are not totally independent of each other, but it is a consideration that apply to all human beings everywhere in the world and at all times in their history.

Before the civil rights era, before the decolonization era, the external variables were fixed and oppressive, and virtually controlled their lives. Since then the external situation has become much more humane, and now one may even argue for their adjustments. Hence, Aframerican social condition has become dominated by effects of the internal variables. Quite likely this is how it will work: the external situation will adjust, then Aframericans move to gain an advantage; the external situation adjusts again, as it will because it is human, and so on indefinitely.

A major problem is going to be, deciding which set of variables is having the controlling influence during a period of interest. How do we know the controlling influences during this period, the beginning of the 21st century? Because there has not been any Aframerican reforms at any time in their history, but importantly, since the decolonization, while there were changes in the external variables, namely civil rights and other laws; we are definitely in the phase requiring Aframerican internal adjustments. Concentrating always on the external situation has this caveat: it will ultimately end up dealing with governmental apparatus, which just so happens to be the internal control mechanism of the opposition or all the opposition combined.

Now, there is a social hierarchy in the Americas and there are social hierarchies throughout the world. As more of the world's peoples are bought into the Americas the global hierarchies are going to be recreated here, and Aframericans will be at the bottom. There is no legitimate way by which government can adjust a community's standing in the hierarchy, so Aframericans are condemned to this position indefinitely if they rely on the state to advance their cause.

Aframerican success at influencing the external situations in the 1960's created the impression that, that is the way to go, but it is a great illusion. Let us take the most celebrated case: the great movement in the United States of America. It was led by Dr. King who has become the symbol for great benevolent social changes, and he is a hero among all Aframerican communities that are aware (some Aframerican communities have not reached the civil rights era in their history yet), but nowhere in the works of Dr. King are there any prescriptions for Aframerican social reforms. His work resulted in the reform of Euro-American societies and was the most important set of reforms in their history in the Americas. They reformed their societies for their own purposes, bringing their practices much more in line with their high principles. On the contemporary world scene, these are the most successful groups of people, ever. It is no wonder that some Aframericans think that nothing has changed, and they are still been oppressed.

Ancient Approach to the Crisis

Nations are generally created by an assembly of wise men and most communities trace their origins, or major modification of their social structure, to some wise man or men. So, it seems to be in the scheme of things that when African Americans perceive a crises in their midst that they began to hold assemblies and conferences to debate and adjudicate on the problems. This approach to social correction we call the 'Mount Sinai method', since it is reminiscent of Moses and his creation of the Israelite nation. The approach has worked wonders for many communities when they required social correction, but it has some serious problems when applied in the 20th century and beyond. There is chiefly the problem of moral authority. The moral authority of most ancient reformers rested on the assertion that they were representatives of a God, and they are recorded as exerting great powers indicating to their contemporaries that God was indeed part of their program. Ancient peoples wanted proof too.

The average individual of modern days is educated beyond the level of ancient sages and they have more than a passing belief in determinism; their lives are dominated by the laws of cause and effect as they function daily in modern society. Unless very great wisdom, knowledge or other capability, far beyond contemporary humans is displayed by the man of God, he is not going to impress anyone. It may be that religious people are the most concerned about Aframerican survival (Aframerican salvation) or theirs is the most popular approach to reform in those communities, whichever is the case, they have held numerous convocations without producing any general schemes that we can follow.

Modern Approach to the Crisis

In the west we believe, and will continue to believe, that sovereignty is derived from the people. This was the chief conclusion that came out of the convulsive process that pervaded Europe during the 17th and 18th centuries. The process that produced the present western democracies was an open and continuous debate for many decades. It is the success of these societies that has put the Aframericans, the Africans and all other peoples in the position of being backward or primitive peoples. It is toward this success that we aspire, sometimes even unwillingly; otherwise we would be content to find some remote retreat, pick berries, and dig for roots. This is not about to happen.

One alternative to the Mount Sinai method is open, continuous debate (democratic consensus) on all the topics that concerns the society in its restructuring. The emphasis here is on debate, not just talking, an injection of reason into the process of our social rehabilitation. We live in an age of explication. Most individuals feel the need to know the wherefore and why of those things that effect their lives. Human beings no longer believe in the right of kings to direct their affairs; neither do they believe in the authenticity of contemporary prophets to do the same. Ultimately then, the people must forge their own destiny. Therefore, they must debate, and exchange points of view, and quarrel, and argue until a consensus is reached. All necessary action then follows this understanding. This is the basic modern approach to government.

If one assumes the existence of a popular (common) goal then after some time a consensus will emerge, otherwise the debate would naturally continue. At this stage the outcome is codified as a social norm. In an Aframerican state it could be backed by law. In a host state it is backed by Aframerican expectations.

Scientific Approach to the Crisis

There is another continuous, discursive, and democratic process that is all pervasive in modern societies. Its success has been overwhelming. This is the process of modern science. Science is open to everyone who is willing to elevate himself or herself to the level of the debate. This reiterative process has elevated all those nations where the people believe in it and damned those who do not. It is inching its way inexorably towards a god-like human greatness.

To keep the scientific debate on track and prevent the whole thing from degenerating into an exchange of personal opinions, a set of self-evident truths are identified; these are the laws of physics. The process of Aframerican rehabilitation requires a similar set of underlying principles or our social debate will degenerate into a series of chats without consequence, dominated by charismatic individuals who will lead us around and around, but produce no permanent philosophy to lead us out of the morass.

The fore going is an overview of the Aframerican situation, the social environment and the limits under which they operate as they seek their own advancement. It is assumed a community seeks only its own interest. The individuals, in their communities, making daily decisions, must be guided by a common thread so that the effect of their activities adds up and are promotional for the group. Each individual is inducted, in childhood, into a regime of preferences and references that constitute a social system and if the totality is not self-promotional then it naturally decays. Aframericans are a new people, their social semblances are without contrivance and cannot work against communities with thousands of years behind them. If they are to survive as a people, there must be an intellectual intervention.

This work aims to initiate the intellectual intervention by identifying a set of clear-cut principles to guide the debate that leads to Aframerican social reform. To legitimately fill this role, the principles need to be simple, "self-evident" to an open mind, and equally applicable to all branches of humanity. The reasoned decisions that ensue from such a debate will form a set of references for the society that produced them. By the above means, we intent to press into service all scientific knowledge of humanity and the historical experiences of the worlds people into making Aframerican rehabilitation the leading branch of the social sciences in the twenty first century.

The Africans were overwhelmed by rising science and industrialism. The present Black population of the Americas are the human byproduct of that process. To a besmirched people such as we are, modern civilization offers a dizzying array of resources via which to transcend our beginnings and rise to global prominence. On the eve of his historic fight with Sonny Liston, Peter Wilson, commentator for the London daily Mirror said of Ali, “Tonight the clown bids to be king”. The rest is history. “Now is time enough, for the Aframerican to leave the spectator stand and step into the ring as a contender”. That is the agenda.

Principles of Social Action

Principle of references

The principle of references state that: no system, or being, biological, mechanical or otherwise, can consistently operate correctly without a reference, or a system of references.

System is used here to mean any functioning apparatus or being. While this principle is as important to engineering as it is to biology and sociology, sociology is where our interest lies.

It is commonly known that sailors travel the seas and guide themselves by the stars; they use the stars as references. They also use the earth's magnetic field. Suppose some one was to set out to cross a large lake where the far side was visible, and suppose he ran into thick fog after starting out but kept on going. It could actually happen that he could turn 180 degrees and not know it until landmarks on the lakeshore were again visible.

A rocket ship, a sailing ship, or a dog walking on a beach would have to have a reference in order to reach a definite destination, otherwise they would get lost. The case of homing pigeons is famous and well-studied; it was mysterious, but it has now been discovered that they use the stars and the magnet field of the earth as their reference.

A simple experiment will serve to demonstrate the social relevance of this principle. Take three pails of water, one that is ice cold, one that is about 40 degrees and another about 65 degrees. Place the right hand into the cold one and the left hand into the hot one for about five minutes. After that, place both hands into the 40-degree pail together. The right hand will feel the water as hot, while the left will feel it is cold. This disagreement arises because the two hands in the same water are using different references.

People are continually making judgments—engineers make measurements—in both cases references are involved. The engineer knows that he cannot make a sensible measurement without a reference which is generally called a standard or unit of measurement.

Individuals generally acquire their references in childhood and just like other factors that they acquire as a child they use them implicitly, often unconsciously. These would be the standards of their community, and when the individual make a judgment, a large number of others are likely to have a similar point of view which gives the impression that the judgment has some kind of general validity—which it does, but only in that community.

The totality of these references forms the basis for a system of preferences, biases, and prejudices that are inherent in every community. They naturally manifest in individual behavior and judgments and are indispensable for normal operation.

Whenever it becomes necessary to consider the structure of human society, or the interaction of societies, it is essential that the role of bias and reference be explicitly understood, otherwise such a debate will, in effect, be just a set of people sequentially speaking, but not actually reasoning together.

The principle of mutual relationships

The principle of mutual relationships states that: for purposes of social action the relationship between individuals is one to one. That is, an individual is as good as another and the principle must apply to communities or it will break down for individuals. The relationship between communities shall be one to one. This is virtually the same condition as is oft quoted from the American declaration of independence, namely: " that all men are created equal, that they are endowed by their creator with certain unalienable rights, that among these are life, liberty and the pursuit of happiness..."

These notions were not self-evident until that time. People in general loved their king/queen and where they did not have one, they created one. Many people have dedicated their lives, and some lost their lives, to ensure the practical application of this principle, and the whole idea is high in the public consciousness.

For this generation of people in the West, adherence to this principle has resulted in a revolution in attitude and actual relationships of most individuals and the process is still going on. For Aframerican practical living these changes are most pronounced. This principle shall produce even grater results. It is instructive to observe that although the United States has many adversaries and antagonist through the world, no politician who wants to be taken serious dares to assert that all men are not created equal.

The conservative principle

Human societies are conservative by nature. People stick to what they know works. A society will not spontaneously reform itself. The natural tendency is to degenerate slowly so people notice what is taking place only over a period of time. Individuals in a community think and act as if they are in a "box" and do not respond to reasoned arguments on why they should change their way of doing things, but they do follow trends. From the point of view of an individual, tradition, culture, custom, trend, fashion, etc., belong to the same class. People do things because other people are doing them. So, the natural way to get things done in human society is to create a trend or movement, which we will call a social current, because it carries people along with it. This gives rise to the social concept of force. Whatever one wants to do to society, if you are not in a movement and you are not trying to create a movement, there is not likely to be any social action on that.

The social principle of force (The conservative principle)

A people, meaning a mass of individuals organized into a people, acts only under the influence of a movement. A movement is a social current. Such influences are emotional in nature; cultures belong to the class of social currents, so that all social currents may be termed temporary or permanent cultures. The existence of cultures pervading among humanity, and functions as the human equivalent of animal instincts, places severe restrictions on the meaning of the individual. A social current then is the social equivalent of what is normally called a force. There is a proportional relationship between the social action and the force that produces it. This relationship is not simple and may not be consistent.

People follow each other like sheep, but they must first be able to see that there is a following. This is all natural and inevitable. Each individual is inducted into a system in childhood and by the time he/she realizes that they have been indoctrinated, it is too late. They have come into being as an inmate of a system; the system that brought them into being. This could cause some dilemma for beings that are very self-conscious.

Social action requires extended exertions. Since such exertions will be resisted, either by conservative forces or conscious forces with their own volition, a struggle will ensue. So that ultimately the processes of social action are through struggle. This is important for those contemplating social action. The results of their efforts will be borne out in statistical effects and you seldom live to see clearly the results.

The universal principle of laws

This principle states that all of creation (existence) is governed by appropriate local or universal laws, irrespective whether these laws are known to humanity or not. The belief in exception to laws, in general or particular, is called caprice.

Creation -the cosmos- has characteristics associated with it such as size, age, and content. Neither the size nor age has been assessed by us with any degree of certainty. The cosmos is so large that its size is irrelevant to us; there is no going to the edge of it. Even the edge of the local galaxy is beyond human reach. Our existence and its relationship to the age of the cosmos is just stimulating intellectual speculation, like our thoughts about its size. The content of the cosmos is much more interesting because some of it is within our grasp, as indeed we are part of it, but its depth (variety of content) may be just as great as its age and size. We are in no position to say what can or cannot be in the cosmos. We find things or phenomena and try to fit then into the known pattern of nature. If we predict something which cannot be found, or visa versa, then we have to modify our beliefs to fit the reality.

Not too long ago, before this age wherein most of humanity accounts for their experience scientifically, resort to caprice was commonplace. Man continually made appeals for special interventions on his behalf in every walk of life; for better weather, better crop yields, more fish in the sea, stronger iron, victory in war, salvation from volcanoes and earthquakes, the list is endless. We did not know, or we did not believe, that the world had a strict inter-relation between its parts that determine the out come of all interactions. In this light, resort to caprice was a common sense course of action.

Quite to the contrary, now we are finding that the laws of nature are inviolable down to the smallest detail that we have been able to test them. The belief in rule of law throughout the cosmos, both local and far, is widely established and spreading. As a consequence, hardly any one asks for an intervention to get a stronger iron. People research to find out how iron gets its strength and then they act according to their findings. This kind of behavior is widely accepted as the normal practice.

Contemporary civilizations emerge almost as a direct result of Isaac Newton's discovery of the laws of motion, as an explicit understanding applying to mechanical or physical nature. Resting on these laws we have gone forth to build steam engines, gasoline engines, rockets engines, walk on the moon, and in some other places that are perhaps more distant, like the depths of the atomic and subatomic world.

About a century ago other thinkers, notably George Boole, found that human thought was also governed by its appropriate laws. By proceeding within the confines of these laws we have gone forth to construct adding machines, industrial controllers and computers; thinking machines.

So we have found that all of nature that we deal with, from the most massive bodies like planets and stars, to the flimsiest most insubstantial existences, like neutrinos and quarks, adhere to the strictest regime of laws. Even the nebulous regions of human thought has its appropriate regiment of laws that govern conduct therein, if out come is to be meaningful and practical. Every time we encounter a new aspect of the cosmos we find that it relates to the rest by strict laws, and it is reasonable to believe that this trend will continue. At various points in the history of our encounter with new natural phenomena, the laws involved are either unknown or poorly understood, thus giving rise to unpredictable cause and effect relationships which at times will be clearly capricious. This only underscores the point that lack of appropriate knowledge is the basis for belief in caprice.

The principle may be stated thus: all aspects of nature interact with the rest under a system of strict natural laws. There is no reason to believe that there is any exemption neither local nor remote. There is one caveat: the totality of the cosmos is not known and is not going to be known by man, so although it is unreasonable to belief in caprice, caprice is possible.

The competitive principle

This principle states that all human beings are in a competition for their life. Socially we compete for quality of life under a gentlemanly system of rules. Sometimes the rules break down, various forms and level of violence break out, and we struggle for existence. The ensuing war or violent confrontations are only heightened states of the competition that was always there.

Living things are continually under attack on the microscopic level and when their defenses fail they are dismantled on that level. They decay; hence, decay is everywhere and ever ongoing. There is an interminable struggle for life as living things deploy an endless array of ingenious strategies on the microscopic level to ward off attacks. They are often under attack on the macroscopic level as well. Each individual ultimately succumbs to the endless invasions, but is replaced by others who carry on the struggle. The competition is all pervasive and is on all levels of life.

Every individual is systematically inducted into a community and inherits the history and the consequences of the history of that community. There is virtually no way out for the individual if local conditions are bad. When and where we cooperate with others it is with those who are believed to be helping us. Individuals strive for advantages over each other; tribes and clans do the same, nations against nations and confederacy of nations exhibit the same behavior. All human beings are involved in the competition for life.

A number of important observations may be made about communities. Every community must have a regime for protecting itself on the microscopic level or it is doomed. It will be penetrated and whatever it is, it is not going to be any more, it will be destroyed.

The individuals in a community are indoctrinated. Inducted into a system in childhood and the vast majority does not have a clue. They really believe their likes and their preferences are really their own. There is no other way. Any community that does not indoctrinate its people is doomed.

Sooner or later, the anxieties of a community will manifest in some of its individuals as paranoia. They are just hypersensitive agents of their communities' concerns. They do not know the wherefore and the why. The largest part of all cultures originates with previous generations, especially the part that concerns human interactions so almost every person on earth is acting out a role handed down to them.

Communities have identified important provisions they feel are critical for their survival. They vary vastly in what is identified. Even if this catalog is arbitrary, as some people imply, the consequences are horrendous. All communities are not created equal, and in competing with each other there are winners and losers. Aframericans are consistently losing. Aframericans are the first and foremost causalities of global industrializations, but could become beneficiaries of the process by using scientific methods and approaches to reform their society; absorb the best competitive measures from all mankind on a global scale. Ultimately the competitive principle is related to, or may be derived from, the law of natural selection.

####

Thank you for reading my book. If you enjoyed it, won't you please take a moment to leave me a review at your favorite retailer?

Thanks.

Piankh

Connect with Me:
mailto: RasPiankh@gmail.com? subject=Organizing the diaspora

Friend me on Facebook: https://www.facebook.com/piankh.piankh
Or contribute directly to the process:
http://www.debate.aframerican.com/index.php
http://bigriver.aframerican.com/

Endnotes

Organizing

Normal societies consist of many overlapping and interlocking subdivisions with many layers. One cannot start from scratch to create such an entity; there is no way to know the full extent of it. Organizing here means advocating, promoting, suggesting, and advising social changes and all people doing any of these or like endeavors are considered to be engaged in organizing activities. Black people in the Western world have their social condition and status under constant deliberation and many people are engaged in corrective actions in their localities. These people are dispersed throughout the twelve million square miles of the Americas and to a lesser degree in Western Europe. Because of this massive dispersion the corrective actions turn out to be a set of random efforts without any coordinating influences (principles). There needs to be a general solution to the "Black peoples" equation that is derived from their internal parameters and the environment under which they operate. Activist who accepts such a solution would have their activities coordinated by it, irrespective of where they are, in space or time.

Diaspora

Here it is intended to mean the African Diaspora, but this is an overarching global phenomenon second only to the dispersion of west European people along a similar time line. They never call themselves the European Diaspora.

Aspect of society

Human societies are systems of loyalties and expectations. The members are inducted during infancy when they depend absolutely on the system and consequently develop faith and loyalty to a similar degree. The average individual never gets beyond the processing. The fact that in some societies quite a few people can see beyond what they have been made into may actually be a part of the programming. Socially, there is hardly anything new under the sun, as asserted by ecclesiastics. Read a variety of ancient text and one will see the same kinds of behavior that we have in our age. The Christian bible, the Mahabharata, Ancient Egyptian text, the Iliad, the Aeneid, tell tales that we can all recognize.

Conspiracies

It really is a grand scale of conspiring and it goes right down to the level of the individual. All over the world people are conspiring to gain advantage—to Aframericans it is a mystery; they generally identify this behavior as racism. Think of a place like India, the people live in tribes in their traditional areas, but even when they are in metropolitan cities like Mumbai (Bombay) their mindset is the same. One can see this in New York or San Francisco easily. If one looks at a city and there is a set of people who are related to each other by kinship, religion, national origin or whatever, and they are essentially operating all the pharmacies, or maybe all the grocery stores or maybe all the gas stations, then they must be conspiring. There is no way they can just incidentally end up in those positions. The people have no choice, what will they do, share their wherewithal with others who know nothing about them or care anything about them. In any case, it is highly regarded; people who behave like that are said to have a tight nit community.

Identity

There is a large number of works on Aframericans, their contemporary condition, and their origin (which determines their identity); but for general information see "Sex and Race," "Africa's Gift to America," and "Great men of Color," all by J.A. Rogers; "Capitalism and Slavery", "Columbus to Castro," by Eric Williams; "Sociology of Slavery in Jamaica", "Slavery and Social Death" by Orlando Patterson; "Anatomy of Racial Inequality," by Glenn C. Loury; "Race and culture" and "conquest and culture," by Thomas Sowell.

In " Anatomy of racial inequality," Lowery succinctly details some African-American situations and proposes some responses. This work is instructive for highlighting the popular African-American mind set in tackling their social ills. He notes in detail how the average African-American seeking some benefit would respond to obstacles in the way of getting what they want. They consistently make negative choices in terms of what they want. His conclusion from this is that the society at large has problems and should set in train a process to correct itself. Any theory that assumes that Aframericans are normal is going to go off course.

The professor's notes also later that the relation between whites and blacks in America goes back to slavery, but does not emphasize that African-Americans have no social history that predates slavery: that is when they originate; that is their defining moment in history and it truly does define them. The ills of Black America are not theirs alone; in South America and the Caribbean the Aframericans are evolving the same kinds of asymmetrical relationships with the Asians that they have with the whites in the North. The Asians came into the Americas in a similar condition to the Aframericans and the latter actually thought themselves a cut above the Asians in many instance. The malignancy of Aframerican origin is not going to go away; it is a permanent part of the picture. They must evolve means of dealing with it at various levels of society and must put something illustrious in the picture to counter its effects.

The works by Sowell, masses tremendous data, clearly showing that the Aframerican situation is found all over the world and is not confined to a special ethnic group (race), nor is caused by a special ethnic group. The synopsis of these works is that throughout human history and geography, people have adopted and adapted material and intellectual wherewithal from each other. The world's most advanced peoples are those who have absorbed most, not always voluntarily. The most backward peoples are those who have absorbed lease for whatever reasons. These reasons vary widely from geographic isolation to their own ability to resist conquest. From these studies, it is clear that no particular set of people, chosen by God or any other agency, from any locality or ethnicity, is locked into place as oppressed or oppressors of humanity.

Dehumanized

This term is often used, but what individuals mean by it is not clear from the way they talk or what they expect from the dehumanized people. It is generally thought that in hierarchy of living things that below the humanity are the animals and above them are the angels or gods. Aframericans were worked like animals, fed like animals, and bred like animals for generations and that was their norm. So they became dehumanized. They were never reconstituted. Of course, they cannot really lose their humanity because it is genetically ordained, but each generation imprints its psychology on the next, thus propagating their oppression indefinitely. The great challenge is how to interrupt this process and supplant it with one that promotes Aframerican advances from within and without.

Conflicting loyalties

Aframericans have an identity problem that goes to the core of their existence. They are all African-something. Some even call themselves Nubians. The average Aframerican knows very little about Africa, speaks no African language, practices no African culture and when they do encounter a genuine Negro, declare the same black and ugly. All their references are European. The Europeans despises Aframericans and by extension Africans. This is evidenced by the method European society uses to designate Aframericans: one drop (1%) of African blood. The Aframericans use the same method, probably for the same reason. In the United states, (and similarly but not quite the same elsewhere), Black society is just an extension of White society, their society does not have a demarcation and so they seek to distinguish themselves by dissenting behavior. This is particularly important to the young who are in the state of becoming. Every generation in society must mold itself in the pattern of some image. Aframericans are in the unenviable position of remaking themselves in the image of people who hurt them and disparaged them on a scale beyond precedence. Do not be surprised if they have problems accepting the identity that they now have.

This is all sentimental; so some people are operating above it, the intellectuals; and some below it, the hedonistic. They operate wherever they see benefit. In between is the average person whose agenda is simply to live and be comfortable. They need definite psychological moorings. That is, they need an identity. Identity is the chief orienting (organizing) vector in a society. It is the one influence that individuals gleefully submit themselves to, and there after become willing to die, to kill and to murder on that basis.

two instances

See, "Conquest and Cultures" or "Race and Culture" by Thomas Sowell.

impervious to their efforts

The Aframerican states found in the Caribbean have among their managers, graduates of the best universities in the world, schooled in current and best economics, but they are all third world countries. There is something going on that is outside the purview of the modern state as it is defined. The same may be said of the religions that they practice. Negative going statistics are to be found among Aframerican population whether they are governed by economics or morality. There are things going on which are outside the scope of contemporary religion. There are numerous groups of Christians who come into the Americas, from far away, strange cultures and do better than Aframericans who have been abed with the worlds leading people for over four centuries. Since Aframerican failures under these circumstances are clearly not the result of any form of intrinsic insufficiency, statistically would not result from apathy, we may conclude that there is some form of systematic resistance taking place. The first guess is that it is something to do with identity.

Competition

Most of the Americas are Christian and those who are churchgoers would be quite familiar with the fact that life on earth has been a struggle from the beginning till now, and it has been a struggle amongst groups of people. Christians may choose to think it is temporary, but it is the only state that humanity actually knows.

Happening every where

Rogers wrote extensively in "Sex and Race" about black populations in various South American countries and what became of them.

Distinguished thinkers

See any standard work on the Atlantic revolution of the seventeenth and eighteenth century or specifically, the works of J.J. Rousseau, Hume, Adam Smith, Hobbes and J.S. Mills.

adapt to the wiles

In America they captioned this behavior in the saying: "They keep moving the goal post." The infamous Rockefeller drug laws of New York State are just blatant examples of a phenomenon which must naturally be occurring everywhere in the United States, and the world in general. This is the position of the majority. The society is just pursuing its own interest (survival) by various tactics. It is not a different phenomenon from that in which Moslems institute" their" laws that turns out to be anti-Christian.

contrive and conspire

As noted before, conspiring is the normal mode of societies and entails social skills that Aframericans must acquire if they are to survive. When confronted with this requirement Aframericans are apt to recoil from what they see essentially as systems of evil practices. They then leave their survival resting on the hope that the strictures that hold various societies together are going to break down, individualism will be pervasive and Aframericans will get justice or attain equality. (When hell freeze over.) This is naive to the extreme, but should not be surprising coming from a people whose history is very short. The various social systems maintained by the world's leading peoples were essential to their survival in ancient times and remain so now. An interesting work reflecting on social cohesion is 'In Praise of Nepotism: A Natural History," by Adam Bellow.

reiterative

This is the master key to all knowledge, it is so simple, belies belief, the beating heart of modern science. Reiteration may be the compliment of the Mount Sinai method as the latter is based on edicts from God, certainty, but the former is based on the not knowing and for admitting that he knew he did not know, Socrates was declared wisest of men. The process is culturally known as trial and error but must be a short hand for "trial and error correction" Error correction is known in engineering as feedback.

<u>Salvation</u>

Means more or less the same as Christians do when they use the word, except this is to be on earth. All the people who survived since ancient times have systems that respond to challenges and challenges are inevitable. Aframerican organizers must look far beyond any contemporary crisis.

hierarchies

Because Aframericans have been at the bottom of the social hierarchy, they can be forgiven for being unable to see that there are such stratifications in every major grouping of people around the world; within race and continents and countries. Some of them have endured for thousands of years and they recur and repeat themselves as these peoples move around the world and set up new communities. This is strongly bought out in "Conquest and Culture" and "Race and Culture" by Thomas Sowell.

Bibliography

The considerations in this work were informed by the following readings, among others.

Kohlenberger, J. R. (1997). The parallel apocrypha: Greek text, King James Version, Douay Old Testament, the Holy Bible by Ronald Knox, Today's English Version, New Revised Standard Version, New American Bible, New Jerusalem Bible. New York: Oxford University Press.

Dawood, N. J. (1978). The Koran. Alan lane Press.

Budge, E. A. (1898). The Book of the dead: The Chapters of coming forth by day, the Egyptian text according to the Theban recension in hieroglyphic, ed. from numerous papyri, with a translation, vocabulary, etc. London: Kegan Paul, Trench, Trübner & Co.

Mishra, T. (2010). The Hindu Book of the Dead. New Delhi: Vitasta Publishing Pvt. Ltd.

Bhagavad-gita As It by His Divine Grace A. C. Bhaktivedanta Swami Prabhupada

The Buddhist Catechism trans. By Henry Steel Olcott

Frazer, J. G., & In Fraser, R. (2009). The golden bough: A study in magic and religion.

Walker, W. (1969). John Calvin.

Hobbes, T. (1962). Leviathan. New York: Dutton.

Lewis, C. S., Simmons, J., & Hoopla digital. (2012). The problem of pain. United States: Harper Collins Publishers.

Bardon, F. (1962). Initiation into hermetics: A course of instruction in ten stages: theory and practice. Kettigüber Koblenz: Osiris-Verlag.

Blavatsky, H. P., & De, Z. B. (1993). The secret doctrine. Wheaton, IL: Theosophical Publishing House.

Blavatsky, H. P. (1923). Isis unveiled. London: Theosophical Publishing House.

Blavatsky, H. P. (2012). From the caves and jungles of Hindostan.

Bailey, A. A. (1973). A treatise on cosmic fire. New York: Lucis Publishing Co.

Bailey, A. (1979). The unfinished autobiography. New York: Lucis Pub.

Bailey, A. A. (2013). A treatise on white magic: Or, The way of the discipline.

Burton, R. E. (1991). Self-remembering. New York: Globe Press Books.

Uspenskiĭ, P. D., & Rosenthal, L. (1994). In search of the miraculous.

Ouspensky, P. D., Maeterlinck, M., & Roel, S. (1947). Tertium organum. Monterrey, N.L: Centro Literario de Monterrey.

Uspenskiĭ, P. D., & Gurdjieff, G. I. (1972). The fourth way: A record of talks and answers to questions based on the teaching of G.I. Gurdjieff [by] P.D. Ouspensky.

Paul, C. K. (1971). Memories. London: Routledge & Kegan.

Gurdjieff, G. I. (1973). Beelzebub's tales to his grandson; or, [An objectively impartial criticism of the life of man]. London: Routledge & Kegan Paul.

Gurdjieff, G. I., Orage, A. R., & Lachman, G. (2015). Meetings with remarkable men.

Haich, E. (1986). Sexual energy and yoga. New York, NY: Aurora Press.

Brunton, P. (2015). The wisdom of the overself.

Bardon, F. (2001). Initiation into hermetics: The path of the true adept. Salt Lake City, UT: Merkur Publishing.

Initiates, T. (2014). The kybalion. New York: Jeremy P. Tarcher.

Russell, B., & Slater, J. G. (1994). Mysticism and logic: Including A Free Man's Worship. London: New York.

Russell, B. A. (1954). The analysis of matter. London: G. Allen & Unwin.

Russell, B. (2012). The analysis of mind.

Russell, B. (2012). Problems of Philosophy. Dover Publications.

Russell, B. (1926). Our knowledge of the external world as a field for scientific method in philosophy. London: Allen & Unwin.

Okadigbo, C. (1985). Consciencism in African political philosophy: Nkrumah's critique. Enugu, Nigeria: Fourth Dimension Publishers.

Comte, A., & Gillespie, W. M. (1851). The philosophy of mathematics. New York: Harper et brothers.

The unreasonable effectiveness of mathematics in the natural sciences by by Eugene Wigner

Nietzsche, F. W., & Mencken, H. L. (2012). The Antichrist.

Nietzsche, F. W., & Rhys, E. (1941). Thus spake Zarathustra. London: Dent.

Mill, J. S., & In Piest, O. (1957). Utilitarianism. New York, [etc.: Macmillan.

Boole, M. E. (1890). Logic Taught by Love: Rhythm in Nature and in Education. London: C. W. DANIEL, 3 Amen Corner, E.C.

DeGroot, J. J. (1977). The religion of the Chinese. Ann Arbor, MI: University Microforms International.

Laozi, & Legge, J. (1997). Tao te ching. Mineola, NY: Dover Publications.

Burton, R. E. (1991). Self-remembering. New York: Globe Press Books.

Hittleman, R. L., & Clear Lake Productions. (1980). Richard Hittleman's yoga for health t.v. series: Introduction to yoga 1-2-3. Santa Cruz, CA: Clear Lake Productions.

Ra, U. N. (1990). Metu Neter, vol. 1: The great oracle Tehuti and the Egyptian system of spiritual cultivation. Bronx, NY: Khamit Corp.

Ra, U. N. (1990). Metu Neter, vol. 1: The great oracle Tehuti and the Egyptian system of spiritual cultivation. Bronx, NY: Khamit Corp.

Ra, U. N. (1994). Metu Neter Vol. 2: Anuk Ausar, The Kamitic Initiation System. Kamit Corp.

Chia, M., & Winn, M. (1984). Taoist secrets of love: Cultivating male sexual energy. Santa Fe, N.M: Aurora Press.

Chia, M. (1981). Awaken healing energy through the Tao: Ancient Chi-Kung : learn how to circulate energy through acupuncture channels by yourself. New York?: Taoist Esoteric Yoga Center & Foundation.

Chia, M. (2009). Fusion of the Eight Psychic Channels: Opening and Sealing the Energy Body . Destiny Books.

Chia, M., & Chia, M. (1990). Iron shirt Chi Kung I: Theory & practice. Huntington, NY: Awaken Healing Light.

Teish, L. (1988). Jambalaya: The natural woman's book of personal charms and practical rituals. San Francisco: Harper & Row.

Saraswati, S., & Avinasha, B. (2002). Jewel in the lotus: The Tantric path to higher consciousness : a complete and systematic course in Tantric Kriya yoga. Valley Village, CA: Ipsalu Tantra.

Chang, S. T., & Chang, S. T. (1992). The Tao of balanced diet: Secrets of a thin & healthy body. San Francisco, CA: Tao Publishing.

Chia, M., Chia, M., & Li, J. (1999). Healing love through the Tao: Cultivating female sexual energy. Hackensack, NJ: Universal Tao Publications.

Bempah, K. (2010). Akan Traditional Religion: The Truth and the Myths . Barnes and Noble.

Burton, R. F. (1854). Late visit to Medina and Mecca: And, Journey from El- Medina to Mecca : [essays].

Gabrieli, F. (2010). Arab historians of the Crusades. London: Routledge.

Massey, G. (1883). The natural Genesis or second part of A book of the Beginnings, containing an attempt to recover and reconstitute the lost origines of the myths and mysteries, types and symbols, religion and language, with Egypt for the mouthpiece and Africa as the birthplace: Vol. 1. London: Williams and Norgate.

Massey, G. (1883). The natural genesis: Or, Secondary part of A book of the beginnings. London: Williams and Norgate.

Gerald, M. (1907). Ancient Egypt the Eye of the world. London.

Henty, G. A. (2009). With Clive in India, or, the beginnings of an empire. Princeton, NJ: Recording for the Blind & Dyslexic.

Roberts, F. S. (1897). Forty-one years in India. London: Bentley.

Russell, R. V., & Hīra, L. R. (1969). The tribes and castes of the Central Provinces of India: In four volumes. Oosterhout: Anthropological Publ.

DAVIS, R. H. (1908). The Congo and Coasts of Africa ... Illustrations from photographs by the author and others. T. Fisher Unwin: London; New York printed.

Stanfield, J. F. (1789). The Guinea voyage. A poem in three books. By James Field Stanfield. London: Printed and sold by James Phillips.

Equiano, O. (1816). The interesting narrative of the life of Olaudah Equiano, etc. Penryn: printed by and for W. Cock.

Burton, R. F. (2007). Land of midian, the: volume 1. BiblioLife.

Burton, R. F. (1879). The land of Midian: (revisited) : Part II. London: C. Kegan Paul.

Dubois W.E.B. (1915). The Negro. University of Pennsylvania Press.

Campbell, M. C. (1990). The Maroons of Jamaica, 1655-1796: A history of resistance, collaboration & betrayal. Trenton, NJ: Africa World Press.

Child, L. M., & Karcher, C. L. (1996). An appeal in favor of that class of Americans called Africans. Amherst: University of Massachusetts Press.

Burton, R. F., & Burton, I. (1964). Personal narrative of a pilgrimage to Al-Madinah & Meccah: Volume 1. New York: Dover Publications Inc.

Burton, R. F., & Burton, I. (1964). Personal narrative of a pilgrimage to al-Madinah & Meccah: Vol. 2. New York: Dover Publ.

Burton, R. F., & Burton, I. (1987). First footsteps in East Africa, or, An exploration of Harar. New York: Dover.

Greaves, A. (2012). Rorke's Drift. Orion.

Jahnke, R. (1997). The healer within: The four essential self-care methods for creating optimal health. San Francisco, Calif.: HarperSanFrancisco.

Sherwood, M. (2007). After abolition: Britain and the slave trade since 1807. London: I.B. Tauris.

Rousseau, & J.-J. (1960). Confessions. London: J.M. Dent.

Sunzi, & Minford, J. (2002). The art of war. New York: Viking.

Russell, B. (1931). Proposed Roads to Freedom; Socialism, Anarchism and Syndicalism, by Bertrand Russell.

Russell, B. (1927). Why I am not a Christian. Touchstone.

Russell, B. (2009). Political ideals. Champaign, IL: BookJungle.

Russell, B. (1964). The practice and theory of Bolshevism. New York: Simon and Schuster.

Russell, B. (1962). Freedom versus organization, 1814-1914. New York: Norton.

Russell, B. (1922). The Problem of China . London: George Allen and Unwin Ltd.

Marshall, A. (1989). Principles of economics: [Hauptbd.]. Düsseldorf: Verl. Wirtschaft u. Finanzen.

Keynes, J. M., & Volcker, P. A. (2016). The Economic Consequences of the Peace. La Vergne: Skyhorse Publishing.

Easterly, W. (2002). The elusive quest for growth: Economists' adventures and misadventures in the tropics. Cambridge, MA: MIT Press.

Smith, A., & Cannan, E. (1950). An inquiry into the nature and causes of the wealth of nations: Vol. 1. London: Methuen.

Colson, C. W., & Pearcey, N. (1999). How now shall we live?: Study guide. Wheaton, IL: Tyndale House Publishers.

Williams, C. (1987). The destruction of Black civilization: great issues of a race from 4500 B.C. to 2000 A.D. Illustrated by Murry N. DePillars. Chicago: Third World Press.

Diop, C. A. (1997). The African origin of civilization: Myth or reality. Chicago, IL: Lawrence Hill Books.

Diop, C. A., Salemson, H. J., & De, J. M. (1991). Civilization or barbarism: An authentic anthropology. Brooklyn, NY: Lawrence Hill Books.

Rogers, J. A. (2014). Sex and Race:Negro-Caucasian Mixing in All Ages and All Lands. Wesleyan University Press.

Rogers, J. A., & Clarke, J. H. (1996). World's great men of color. New York: Touchstone.

ROGERS, J. A. (1989). AFRICA'S GIFT TO AMERICA. HELGA M. ROGERS.

Rogers, J. A. (2015). From superman to man.

Rogers, J. G. (1952). Nature knows no color-line: Research into the Negro ancestry in the white race. New York: J.A. Rogers.

James, G. M. (1954). Stolen Legacy.

James, C. L. (1938). The black Jacobins. NY: The Dial Press.

Du, B. W. (1990). The souls of black folk. Charlottesville, VA: American Studies at the University Virginia.

Du, B. W. (1973). The suppression of the African slave-trade to the United States of America 1623-1870. Millwood, N. Y: Kraus-Thomson.

Washington, B. T., & Du, B. W. (2011). The Negro in the South, his economic progress in relation to his moral and religious development: Being the William Levi Bull lectures for the year 1907. Philadelphia: G.W. Jacobs & Co.

Frazier, E. F., & Platt, A. M. (2001). The Negro family in the United States. Notre Dame, IN: University of Notre Dame Press.

Wood, J. T., NetLibrary, Inc, & University of Virginia. (1996). The capture of a slaver. Charlottesville, VA: University of Virginia Library.

Garraty, J. A. (1968). The history of the United States: A history of men and ideas. London: Allen Lane.

Nutting, A. (1994). Scramble for Africa: The great trek to the Boer War. London: Constable.

Thornton, A. P. (1985). The imperial idea and its enemies : a study in British power. Macmillan.

Hill, N., & McConnohie, M. (2006). Think and grow rich: The 21st-century edition. Arden, NC: Highroads Media.

Carnegie, D. (2008). How to win friends and influence people. Princeton, NJ: Recording for the Blind & Dyslexic.

Opokuwaa, N. A. (2005). Akan protocol: Remembering the traditions of our ancestors. New York: Authors Choice Press.

Garvey, A. J. (1977). Philosophy and opinions of Marcus Garvey. New York: Atheneum.

Williams, E. E. (2003). From Columbus to Castro: The history of the Caribbean, 1492-1969. London: Deutsch.

Williams, E. E., & Brogan, D. W. (1964). Capitalism [and] slavery. London: A. Deutsch.

Williams, E. E. (1994). British historians and the West Indies. Brooklyn, NY: A & B Books.

Roberts, G. W., & University of the West Indies (Mona, Jamaica). (1975). Fertility and mating in four West Indian populations: Trinidad and Tobago, Barbados, St. Vincent, Jamaica. Mona], Jamaica: Institute of Social and Economic Research, University of the West Indies.

King, M. L. (2010). Why we can't wait.

Carmichael, S., & Hamilton, C. V. (1992). Black power: The politics of liberation in America. New York: Vintage Books.

X, M., & Breitman, G. (1993). Malcolm X speaks: Selected speeches and statements. New York [u.a.: Pathfinder.

Davis, A. Y. (1975). Angela Davis—an autobiography. New York: Bantam Books.

Nkrumah, K. (2002). Ghana: The autobiography of Kwame Nkrumah. London: Panaf.

Marx, K., & Engels, F. (1967). The Communist manifesto. Harmondsworth, Middlesee: Penguin Books.

Shipside, S., & Marx, K. (2009). Karl Marx's Das kapital: A modern-day interpretation of an economic classic. Oxford, U.K: Infinite Ideas.

Rothbard, M. (2013). Anatomy of the state. Raleigh, NC: Lulu.com.

Russell,B.(1927). Why I Am Not a Christian, Watts & Co., for the Rationalist Press Association Limited.

Faucher, L. (1852). Léon Faucher,"Property I (2013 ed.).

Russell, B. (1978). Free thought and official propaganda. New York: B.W. Huebsch.

Mill, J. S. (2016). On Liberty. Lanham: Dancing Unicorn Books.

Alexander, C. A. (1965). Henry David Thoreau's Walden: And, On the duty of civil disobedience. New York: Monarch Press.

Steers, R. M. (1999). Made in Korea: Chung Ju Yung and the rise of Hyundai. New York: Routledge.

Micklethwait, J., & Wooldridge, A. (2005). The company: A short history of a revolutionary idea. New York: Modern Library.

Hubbard, L. R., & Sherr, L. (2007). Dianetics: The modern science of mental health. Los Angeles, CA: Golden Era Productions.Paine, T. (1792). Rights of man: Part the second. London: Printed for H.D. Symonds.

Paine, T. (1987). Common sense, and other political writings. New York: Macmillan.

Blackmon, D. A. (2008). Slavery by another name: The re-enslavement of Black Americans from the Civil War to World War II. New York: Doubleday.

Spencer, H. (2014). The Right to Ignore the State. Auckland: The Floating Press.

Rousseau, J.-J, & Liberty Fund. (2008). The Social contract: And Discourses. London: J.M. Dent & Sons, Ltd.

Oppenheimer, F., & Gitterman, J. M. (2016). The state: Its history and development viewed sociologically. United States: CreateSpace Independent.

Sowell, T. (1994). Race and culture: A world view. New York: Basic Books.

Sowell, T., & Sowell, T. (1998). Robert Sowell, author, "Conquests and cultures: an international history.".

Sowell, T. (1995). The vision of the anointed: Self-congratulation as a basis for social policy. New York: BasicBooks.

Sowell, T., & Recorded Books, Inc. (2009). Black Rednecks & White Liberals. New York: Encounter Books.

Sowell, T. (2002). The Quest for Cosmic Justice. New York: Simon & Schuster.

Ethnic America: A History by Sowell, Thomas

Sowell, T. (2007). A conflict of visions: Ideological origins of political struggles. New York, NY: Basic Books.

Baxter, P., & Sansom, B. (1973). Race and social difference: selected readings. Baltimore: Penguin.

Loury, G. C., & Ebrary, Inc. (2003). The Anatomy of Racial Inequality. Cambridge: Harvard University Press.

Hebron, M. E. (1966). Motivated learning: A developmental study from birth to the senium. London: Methuen.

Hertz, D. S. (2009). How Jews became Germans: The history of conversion and assimilation in Berlin. New Haven, CT: Yale University Press.

Gibson, K. (2003). The cycle of racial oppression in Guyana. Lanham, MD: University Press of America.

Kim, E. M. (1999). Big business, strong state: Collusion and conflict in South Korean development, 1961-1990. Albany, NY: State University of New York Press.

Rogers, J. A. (1970). \100\one hundred\ amazing facts about the Negro: With complete proof : a short cut to the world history of the Negro. New York, NY: Helga M. Rogers.

Herbert, F. P. (1984). Dune: Book one in the Dune chronicles. New York: Berkley.

Appiah, P., & Dickson, M. (1989). Tales of an Ashanti father. Boston: Beacon Press.

Shakespeare, W. (2004). Shakespeare, complete works: English & German. Berlin: Directmedia Publ.

Sophocles, & Hadas, M. (1988). The complete plays of Sophocles. New York: Bantam.

Homer, Rees, R., & Butler, S. (1998). The Iliad. San Bruno, CA: Audio Literature.

Homer, & Rees, E. (1960). The Odyssey. New York: Random House.

Virgil, & Douglas, G. (1964). Aeneid. Edinburgh: Printed for the Society by W. Blackwood.

Ovid, & Riley, H. T. (1919). Metamorphoses. London: G. Bell.

Carter, J., & Hoopla digital. (2008). A remarkable mother. United States: Simon & Schuster Audio.

Achebe, C. (1900). Things fall apart. Worcester: School for the Blind.

Burton, R. F., & Newby, P. H. (1958). The book of the thousand and one nights: [translated] by Sir R. Burton. London: Barker.

Seacole, M. (2014). Wonderful adventures of Mrs Seacole in many lands. Cambridge: Cambridge University Press.

An essay on the American contribution and the democratic idea by Winston Churchill (1)

Higginson, T. W., & Amazon.com (Firm). (2005). Black rebellion: Five slave revolts : a selection from Travellers and outlaws. Place of publication not identified: Public Domain Books.

Henty, G. A. (1880). By Sheer Pluck: A Tale of the Ashanti War. London: Blackie and Son Limited.

Haggard, H. R. (2011). Cetywayo and his White Neighbours Remarks on Recent Events in Zululand, Natal, and the Transvaal. Hamburg: tredition.

International Center for Research on Women (ICRW), UNICEF. (2015). Child Marriage, Adolescent Pregnancy and Family Formation in West Central Africa.

Ora Martin, Inc, & Stowe, H. B. (1925). Coming: Ora Martin, Inc., Uncle Tom's cabin. United States: Ora Martin, Inc.

Stockwell, J. (1978). In Search of Enemies: A CIA story. London: Deutsch.

Klass, M. (1996). Singing with Sai Baba: The politics of revitalization in Trinidad. Prospect Heights: Waveland.

Neyland, J. (1992). George Washington Carver. Melrose Square, Los Angeles.

Reinl, H., Däniken, E, Terra Filmkunst, & VCI Home Video (Firm). (1977). Chariots of the gods. United States: VCI.

Fiot, J., & Voltaire. (1991). Candide. Vanves, France: Hachette.

Don't miss out!

Visit the website below and you can sign up to receive emails whenever Piankh Piankh publishes a new book. There's no charge and no obligation.

https://books2read.com/r/B-A-EKVM-TLYIB

BOOKS 2 READ

Connecting independent readers to independent writers.

Did you love *Organizing the Diaspora*? Then you should read *Reconstruction: African American*[1] by Piankh Piankh!

[2]

The purpose of this work is to draft a broad course that makes the reform of African American society look straight forward. There are complexities in the details, but they are the responsibility of the individuals who carry out the work and not visionaries such as this author. In the African American population there are diverse views concerning what to do, what is important to do and what to do first. This essay is inspired by the belief that African American society has been losing ground in the great competition and must reform in order to survive. Members of the community needs to initiate a series of adjustments among themselves, that can be known and so can be practiced, to become their system of "national salvation". This means

1. https://books2read.com/u/mBwEOk

2. https://books2read.com/u/mBwEOk

changes in the group dynamics, it is not an issue of one or the other individual, black individuals can survive anywhere; USA, Germany, China, Pakistan, etc. but it is widely accepted that a community of their kindred and culture is the best place for them to survive.

Humanity has made great technical and scientific progress but has also made advancements in social affairs. The progress remains impressive, so much so, it overwhelms some people's judgment, they think the millennium has arrived and begin to advocate individualism as the way of life. All such advocates have been carried away and have forgotten that human beings are animals, and most of their achievements are to satisfy their animal drives. When we contrast this with the "spiritual" achievements, we see that those come through deprivation and sacrifice, not the glory of conquering nature, science, or men. This leads us to believe there will be a contradiction in all physical benevolence, from friend or foe.

On achieving a credible movement towards African American reform, there will be naysayers and "Luke-warm" participants. We should waste no energy on them, their beliefs mean they have no direction, no zeal and no hope in themselves. We only need to "keep the faith" and keep the organization intact. They will pass away, and the organization will induct their children.

We cannot, under any circumstances, abandon our own good to others. Rather, all humanity must strive together, towards the good; together.

Also by Piankh Piankh

Aframericanism
Organizing the Diaspora

Standalone
A Short Treatise on the Space-Time Continuum
Reconstruction: African American

www.ingramcontent.com/pod-product-compliance
Lightning Source LLC
LaVergne TN
LVHW090129160826
845673LV00015B/1126

* 9 7 8 1 6 3 7 9 5 1 0 6 4 *